Executive Producers: John Christianson and Ron Berry
Art Design: Gary Currant
Layout: Currant Design Group and Best Impression Graphics

by Marcia Leonard
illustrated by Bartholomew

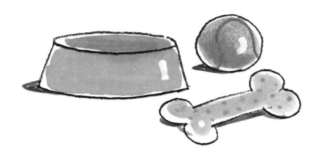

This little girl is pretending
to be a puppy.
She likes being silly.

These kids like being silly, too.
They're having a good time
clowning around outside.

When this little boy feels silly,
he makes funny faces.

Have you ever done that?
Can you make a face that looks silly?

When these little girls feel silly,
they make funny sounds.

Can you make up silly words, too?

There are times when it's okay to be silly,
and times when it's not.

Does this look like a good time to be silly?

There are places where it's good to be silly,
and places where it's not.

Do you think this is a good place?

If you are silly at the wrong time or place,
you might bother other people.

And if your silliness gets too wild,
someone might even get hurt.

You can have a loud and bouncy,
giggly good time when you feel silly.

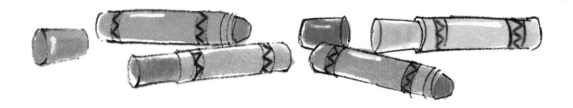

But after a while,
it's good to take time out
for some quieter fun.

MAKE A FACE
Instructions

Use the Make-a-Face activity found in the back of this book to help your child identify and express a whole range of feelings. Remove the chart and reusable stickers from the pocket. Ask your child to make a face by placing stickers on the chart. Then help him or her identify the emotion it expresses. Does the face look scared, angry, happy, or just plain silly? Construct another face with the stickers and talk about what it shows. Try having your child look in the mirror and make a variety of faces.